Adam Taylor has performed his
at the South Bank, at arts
International Poetry Festival and the Edinburgh Festival fringe,
at other literary and cultural events, comedy clubs and schools.
Now living in London, the Dublin-born poet has been
published and featured in national newspapers including *The
Sunday Times* and *The Independent*, as well as poetry magazines
such as *Poetry Review* and *Orbis*. He was poet in residence at
Yahoo.

Adam Taylor

God's face in your gazpacho

Matador
9 De Montfort Mews
Leicester LE1 7FW, UK
Tel: (+44) 116 255 9311 / 9312
Email: books@troubador.co.uk
Web: www.troubador.co.uk/matador

ISBN 978-1905886-814

Typeset in 12pt Bembo by Troubador Publishing Ltd, Leicester, UK
Printed in the UK by The Cromwell Press Ltd, Trowbridge, Wilts, UK

Matador is an imprint of Troubador Publishing Ltd

To my family

Contents

IV

V

VI

I

On 14 August 1940 the Daily Express reported that Mrs Betty Tylee and Miss Jean Smithson approached a downed German pilot. They declined to shoot him and instead offered him a cup of tea.

Will You Shoot Me Now?

No, we don't do that in England
said Mrs Betty Tylee
would you like a cup of tea?
Though one thing we do do
is put milk in first.

The military police
aren't due until three
said Miss Jean Smithson
as she rummaged in
the biscuit tin.
Gosh, your Messershmitt's in
a bit of a mess.

Not to mention my garden
said Mrs Betty Tylee
unsmilingly.
Here's a teaspoon.
Cheers.

Then she stabbed him with
her garden shears.

The Art of Leadership

We hugged
and slapped high fives
like it said in the book.

NOW THE VIM THING, I shouted
THE VIM THING? she screamed.
VISION, I shouted
VISION, she screamed.
INSPIRATION, I shouted
INSPIRATION, she screamed.
MOMENTUM, I shouted
MOMENTUM, she screamed.
THAT'S THE VIM THING, I shouted
THE VIM THING, she screamed.

We hugged
and slapped high fives
like it said in the book.

Then my cleaning lady
went back to work.

Sick Home Syndrome

The door is alarmed.
The roof is aloof.

The floor is bored.
It feels ignored
just like the records.

The mirror's reflecting
on a life of deflection.

The table's groaning
but not with food
or delicacies.

There's a certain malaise
amongst the trays.

The toilet's flushed
but the curtains are pale
and drawn.

The welcome mat
needs a new "e"

and my house could do
with a dose of feng shui.

Elsewhere

A man walks
into a room
which isn't a place
where no-one is
or where he is;
it's a space
where she's not
because he wants
or at least expects her
to be there.
But she isn't.

A woman walks
into a room
which isn't a space
where no-one is
or where he's not;
it's a place
where she is
because she neither wants
nor expects him
to be there.
And he isn't.

Nth Degree

He graduated
summa cum laude
phi beta kappa
frat sororitate
cum magnum
et magnificus
et mirabilus
et benedictus
et spiritus sanctus

in sales and marketing

Discuss.

A train leaves London
at ten am
averaging 90.

A bluish train
bisected by
a purple stripe
ambles out
of Liverpool Lime
in a gentle arc;
it's too late
and of nearly eight
per cent on board
wearing glasses,
a proportion
is vegetarian
but not vegan
though she was once.

No one gets off at Crewe
but a man
from Education
gets on
with pencil, notebook
and a Tesco's bag
with seven apples
and some pears.

The trains stop
five yards apart.
Drivers chat.
Travellers mingle.
Pimms is served.
A quartet plays.
Three waltz.
Two well.

The man from Education
vows next time
he'll take the bus.

Discuss.

Dot Dot Dot

… by a pointillist
so it consists
entirely of dots
and a minimalist
so only three …

… not so much *nice,*
as delightfully concise,
a triptych,
basic maybe,
yet epic, rhetorical…

…fearlessly bare,
atomic,
molecular,
microcosmic…

… eyes and a nose,
ears and a mouth?
the blind mice?
the musketeers?...

…a lot to the eye
but joining them
isn't advised…

…something I
could've done
but didn't…

…a synopsis
of four?...

…(an ellipsis)
or more?...

dot dot dot

It took Ingres 12 years to complete his portrait of Madame Moitissier. "My enemy", he called it. He had to repaint her dress three times because the existing one kept going out of fashion.

My Enemy

For hour after hour
While she sat in that chair
He assessed the effect
Of the light on her hair

He weighed up dimensions
Of height, depth and space
And how they informed
The contours of her face

During the series
Of preparatory sessions
Mademoiselle tried
A range of expressions

Seriously haughty
Yet somehow mysterious
Impish and naughty
With a dash of imperious

After some months
Of toil and trial
He decided to go for
The enigmatic smile

★ ★ ★

He dabbed and he daubed
With pigments and dyes
And slowly the painting
Materialised

Brimming with subtle
Yet pointed motifs
Later much copied
In Al Fresco's reliefs

Two little old men
And two larger old ladies
Playing bridge on the bridge
On the ferry to Hades

In their wake rose an oyster
Seated inside, the pearl
This embodiment of
The essence of girl

A reincarnation
Of divine Aphrodite
Barely attired
In a gossamer nightie

Her youth would stay frozen
Pale and sublime
Despite the relentless
Dripping of time

Those period features
Delicately chiselled
Would never be crinkled
Or jaded or grizzled

★ ★ ★

They came from afar
To the unveiling party
The crème de la crème
Of French literati

Anxious to see
The masterful oeuvre
Before it was carted
Off to the Louvre

One of those present
Was Toulouse Lautrec
He wasn't invited
He'd showed up on spec

In the midst of the throng
Stood Mademoiselle
Having just lately
Emerged from her shell

Indifferent to
The froing and toing
The sighs and the gasps
The aahing and oohing

So they asked her, please tell us
Don't you like what you see?
She said, it really isn't
A good one of me

So the painter went home
And opened a beer
Then cut off his ear

II

God's Face Appeared in your Gazpacho

God's face appeared
in your gazpacho –
a refreshing mosaic
of red pepper ears
and slightly surprised
cucumber eyes
weeping tears
of chopped tomato.

The sun didn't change
its normal course.
No neighbours came
nor ailing masses
nor men of god
to check in light
of latest doctrine.

God's face appeared
in your gazpacho –
but you never knew.
You'd mislaid
your reading glasses.

In Sir Stanley Spencer's 1920 painting "Christ Carrying The Cross", Jesus is shown walking down the main street in Cookham on Thames, Berkshire.

When Jesus Came to Cookham

When Jesus came to Cookham
he strolled down
the main street
for three minutes
one Saturday morning
without warning.
Mrs Hazlitt
from the bookshop
couldn't quite
place the face.

When Jesus came to Cookham
no one knew
quite what to do.
One person gathered
in the church
where the priest advised
against a sacrifice
whether animal
or otherwise.

When Jesus came to Cookham
it took him
three minutes
to realise
he'd come too soon.
So he left
carrying a case
in the shape of a cross.

Gone

"I'm off", he said.
And with that
he was gone.

Like something
that was here once
but isn't any more.

Like the Incas.

Or a pea
that's rolled under
the fridge.

Or a spider
that's been flushed down
the toilet.

Or someone
who's just delivered
a pizza.

Or a pizza
that's just been eaten

except for a crumb
that's been taken by spaceship
to the edge of the time
and space continuum
and kicked out
into nothingness.

And then he came back
with the newspaper.

The Day Mr Audley Decided to Become a Free Spirit

Got up lateish.
Had three cups of tea
instead of the usual two.
Transcendentally
meditated
while waiting
for the eggs to boil.
Made a packed lunch
and wrapped it
asymmetrically
in foil.

Donned sandals
and socks
and a loincloth
from M&S
which was decorated
with leaves
and berries.

Cut off the sleeves
of his anorak.
Painted a skull
on the back.
Put it on.
Finished the crossword.
And was gone.

At the press conference his wife
made a tearful plea
for him to return
and mend
the garden fence.

So he did.

Caged

The rhythm slithers
off the stage,
no longer caged
it's on the run.
Mrs Eileen Dempsey
in 21C
is first to succumb
discreetly drumming
the bag on her lap.

The rhythm's rampaging,
the mayor is grooving
in a kind of a way,
the Partington sisters
furtively sway
and energised by
an earlier nap
Mr Alistair Parfitt
bursts into a hum.

The rhythm is rushing
up to the head
of Dr Gore-Blyth.
His blood cells perform
a Mexican Wave
an intravenous rave
right down to his feet
which spontaneously tap
in time to the beat.

The rhythm is clutching
the frozen shoulders
of the begrudgers.
Row 39
is watching the floor
its silent screams
completely ignored
the rhythm nudges it
to centre stage.

The rhythm's battering
into the wall
of folded arms
relentlessly like
a persistent alarm
it steps up its attack
on Row 39.
The Maginot Line
is starting to crack.

The rhythm is gushing
in through the gap.
No longer trapped
we're up off our seats
and we're clapping
and rapping
and jiving
and writhing
and slapping high fives.

The rhythm subsides.
The Pied Piper has gone.
Mr Jeremy Gageby
insurance broker
of Gageby & Co
disengages the elbow
of Jennifer Jopling
from around his throat.
He puts on his coat.

And Row 39
climbs back in its cage.

3am

3am,
Milan airport.
A bruised green suitcase
with initials OR
miserably circles

Every 45 seconds
it passes through
a box of light
from an office window
where a baggage official
phones his girlfriend.

3am,
Hotel Los Alamos
near Torremolinos
which has a bar called
The Pub.

Mr Oliver Rathbone
of Stow on the Wold
turns off the light
and for the first time ever
he gets into bed
without his pyjamas.

In a Car Boot Sale

His briefcase.
His braces.
Some shirts.

A cert
from Eastbourne Poly
marking his
discovery of
the 18th biggest
prime number
known to man.

His watering can.

A letter to M&S
complaining that
the lack of cardigans
in summer was silly
because you need one
on the beach
when it's chilly.

His socks.
Some earmuffs.
A box
of assorted cufflinks.

Sixty five
return tickets
to Mablethorpe.
And the sixty sixth.
Unused.

The spotted bowtie
he used to wear
on weekly outings
to the car boot sale.

Standard

a standard birth
a standard school
a standard job
a standard wife
standard tension
a standard dog
a standard commute
a standard drink
in a standard pub
standard strife
a standard pension
a standard illness
a standard hospital
a standard death

of course he was fully insured
with Standard Life

The Sydenham Branch

when stock markets crash

    there
    concrete and rational
    is the Sydenham branch
    of the Abbey National

        not perhaps
        an icon of fashion
        or a focus of passion

            although many are fond
            of its Guaranteed Bond

A Visionary with Credibility

We are renowned
for leveraging
state of the art
people
and solutions
with audacious flair
in East Anglia
where we're a major player
supplying workers
and bricks
and spades
to the building trade.

Here's the deal.

All on our own
we've just developed
brick-a-block,
an innovative
preformed
structural
walling system.

It's an exciting alternative
to conventional
blockwork construction.

So we're a business
poised for growth
for which you'll be
the catalyst
and strategist

because you command
instant respect,
your inspired
interpersonal skills
perhaps acquired
as leader of
a religious sect.

In a previous life
you might have
brought your people
to the Promised Land
or drawn a line
in the sand
and made speeches
about fighting them
on the beaches
or perhaps
you conquered Gaul
or even better
built a Great Wall.

So please apply.

Because we need you
to tell us
what the hell
we ought to do.

Hairs to You

Hairs to You
for a top class haircut
in your own home.

We also offer
first class chat.
Topics include
an indiscretion
by a certain person
which has come
to our attention.

Why not sample
our hairdrying service
featuring
our new
5 speed hairdryer
20p per minute
or part of a minute.

Hairs to You.
Fourth place
Suffolk
Blowdrying Finals
1995.
Third place
Avant Garde
Hair Competition
1989.

Call Carol
02727 623450
Mornings
Afternoons
Evenings
Or nights.

Hairs to You.
Mobile hairdressers
By Appointment
to the Crown
and Duck
on the High Street.

Hairs to You.

"Say Yes to the Yenton" is the slogan of the Yenton, a two-star hotel in Bournemouth.

Say Yes to the Yenton

So many reasons
to Say Yes to the Yenton,
the Hotel For All Seasons
where a trouser press
is available
on request.

Say Yes
to a warm greeting
from smiling staff
and award winning
central heating.

Say Yes to the Yenton,
a Piece of Country
in the Heart of Town.
Our rustic grounds
rolling down to the river
teem with wildlife.
Birds, for example
and squirrels
and insects
too numerous
to mention
here.

Say Yes
to twenty two
well groomed bedrooms

overlooking
our rustic grounds.
All equipped
with stylish
clothes hangers
of various shapes
to suit all tastes.

Say Yes to the Yenton
where well behaved dogs
are accepted
by prior arrangement
but not in public rooms
or rustic grounds.
And owners must pay
for any biting
or chewing
of soft furnishings
by dogs

or owners.

Many comment on
Restaurant La Yenton,
so romantic at night
its subtle lighting
gently falling
on Grecian figurines,
enviously eyeing
culinary delights
delicately prepared
by our chef de cuisine
who has visited France
three times.

Children may choose
half portions
or the Yenton
'Juniors' menu
for under eights.
Proof of age needed.

Why not say Yes
to a relaxing drink
after your meal
with friends
old and new
in Mac's Bar.
Overlooking
our rustic grounds.
It's spacious, elegant,
tastefully refurbished
in traditional style.
It's an ideal spot
to contemplate
evening shadows
creeping over
our rustic grounds.

Say Yes to the Yenton.
We've spent an
awful lot of money
to keep it in peak condition
to your complete satisfaction
from fresh redecoration
in the low season
to minor daily repairs
as and when required.

Say Yes to the Yenton
where
according to
our visitors book
Twenty July
Nineteen Seventy Nine
Mr and Mrs
P Harris
had a really nice time.

Say Yes to the Yenton.

III

Dog Eat Dog

Analyst ask why.
Dog say hungry.
Analyst say your flesh and blood.
Dog say I know. I not proud.
Analyst ask about puppyhood.
Dog say tough. Not enough food. Dog eat dog.
Analyst say ah. That's why dog eat dog.
Dog say thanks.
Dog pay.
Dog go home.
Dog hungry.
Dog eat dog.

On Wildebeests

The acidic cold
of the Masai Mara
at dawn.

Little groups of wildebeests.
Huddling,
chatting quietly,
limbering up,
stretching,
yawning,
contemplating the day ahead.

As the sun rises.
Strolling,
trotting,
galloping,
breaking into
a bit of a stampede.

A psychiatrist might ask
if they're running away from their responsibilities.
But in fact they're running away
from animals
who like to feast

on wildebeests.

Because

because it's fun
because it's cool
because it's done
because I'm fast
because I'm smart
because I'm bored
because it bonds us
because it gets me out
because I want to
because I should
because I must
because he's lost it
because he wants it
because he's lost it again
because it's a stick
and I'm a dog
and that's the way it is

Meat Soup

To your average piranha
it's all the same.
A man, a
dog, a lamb chop.
It's all meat.
Still,
quite a treat.

Piranha
are not fabled
for their table manners.
No time for grace.
It's all a race.

Flashing just
the odd tail or fin,
they tuck straight in.
And soon
the water's red,
it bubbles and froths
like overdone
tomato broth.

But god
put a spanner
in the works
when he created
a vegan piranha
called Anna.

And if you meet her
I suggest you throw her
a banana.

A Worm's Lament

It's disconcerting
when I open the curtains
and I can't tell
which end of me
is which.

The Moth: A Warning

Don't incur
the wrath of a moth.
especially if
you're a man of the cloth.

IV

Poem of Atonement

we have slandered
we have robbed
we have bribed
we have wrought wickedness
we have lied
we have provoked
we have trespassed
we have transgressed
we have oppressed
we have rebelled
we have abominated
we have wallowed in evil

but otherwise we think
we've done quite well

The Jewish Singles Do

He said hi
She said hello
He said some grape juice? There's red or white
She said no thank you
He said do you know Simon Levy?
She said just to say hello to
He said me too –
    so did you go to the Young Friendship do at the Spiro?
She said the tomato tasting?
He said yes
She said no
He said it was so so. Simon Levy was there
She said oh
He said Michelle Cantor was there too –
    I took her on a blind date once
She said so?
He said not great. She brought her mate –
    anyway what do you do?
She said I specialise in 16th century art at Sotheby's. You?
He said I'm in computers. So is Simon Levy
She said really
He said I like art. You know the ones of the dripping clocks?
She said yes
He said maybe we could discuss them over dinner?
She said maybe
He said my name is Jeremy
She said I know
He said oh?
She said we met a year ago. I was the mate on that date –
    don't you remember?
He said uh oh. Anyway what's your number?
She said I've no phone

He said well, what the hell, let's elope
She said nope

A prehistoric creature called Acanthostega used to live in muck at the bottom of the sea, waiting for food to swim by. It had a salamander-like body with big glassy eyes on top of a flat Muppet style head. Acanthostega was the earliest known vertebrate lifeform that crawled out of the sea to live on land about 400 million years ago.

Adam

I'm Adam the Acanthostega.
My quality of life's quite meagre.
Lurking on the Atlantic shelf
I feel I can't express myself.
There's little point in being ambitious
when all you meet are ancient fishes.

On reaching land – if I could make it –
I'd run around completely naked.
Then settle down and find a wife
and venture out to get a life.
Once I'd evolved a little more
I'd open an account offshore.

I'm Adam the Acanthostega.
I'm feeling pressured and beleaguered.
Skulking underneath the oceans
I can't tune in to my emotions.
I try to share with my pal Bob.
Sadly, he's just a primitive blob.

I did once date an alligator.
She was a poor communicator.
I said, you'll soon get over me.
There are plenty others in the sea.
She smiled; meanwhile her tail went splat
and ever since my head's been flat.

I'm Adam the Acanthostega.
Plumbing depths of around one league, ugh
can't stand this dirt and filth and grime
the mud, the muck, primeval slime.
I'd really love to power shower
and spray myself with passionflower.

Then out to dine, a top class venue
but please no seafood on the menu.
I've always had first rate relations
with lobsters, crabs and other crustaceans.
Though I wouldn't mind a glass of wine
to take away the taste of brine.

I'm Adam the Acanthostega.
I've never been to Leeds or Riga.
The Seven Wonders of the World
are to me like a flag that's furled.
These torpid hours concealed in murk
would drive any vertebrate berserk.

I sometimes visit that rock there.
I go by sea and not by air.
It isn't much of a vacation,
so little chance for recreation.
As skiing doesn't yet exist
I'm feeling terribly off piste.

I'm Adam the Acanthostega.
Not second rate, I'm a premier leaguer.
I lead my cohorts from the fore.
So I'm the first to crawl ashore.
As I later mentioned to my daughter,
the first ever fish that's out of water.

And I find the fresh air very taxing.
So I build a deck chair to relax in.
But someone's made it here before us
and I don't mean a dinosaurus.
When I return to my deck chair
a German towel is already there.

The Sacrifice of Isaac

god's command

a tortured father
an eternal journey
a loyal son

an expectant altar
a readied pyre
a flashing knife

a sudden angel
a last minute reprieve
a father's relief

an unlucky sheep

A bumper sticker says: "Jesus is coming. Look busy."

The Messiah is Coming

Cancel milk
Defrost meat
Delete files
Learn Hebrew
Wash your hands
Wash his feet
Make blessing
Build temple
Sacrifice sheep
Sacrifice goats
Sacrifice Isaac
Reassess life
Delve into soul
Eat

Location, Location

The Messiah landed
at two am
local time
in a gilded chariot
flanked
by burning questions:
Is this the end of then?
The start of now?
The rebirth of wow?
Might Armageddon come soon?
Or Apocalypse later?
What of processions
and resurrections?
Will he reveal
a universal truth?
And where were you
when you first heard the news?

Don't Mess with Us

Show them a sign but

nothing that might
get out of hand,
no mountains
skipping like rams
or hills like lambs.

nothing that swarms
or hops or bites,
no locusts or lice
and please don't infringe
any animal rights.

nothing distasteful
or politically
incorrect, no need
to call in
the Angel of Death.

nothing that's stale,
no moving statues –
too clichéd, and tears
and rivers of blood
are passé.

Show them

something novel,
fresh and original,
not resurrection –
that's been done.

something that shows
but doesn't tell
yet pointed, insistent
and verifiable
by Ernst and Young.

something that hints
at a Mr Big, a Godfather
who owes us a favour
and is tough but fair.
Though not entirely.

something that says
we have a friend
who's bigger than you

don't mess with us.

Helpline

I covet my neighbour's ox.
So I phone my rabbi
who says it's more normal
to desire
one's neighbour's wife.

I take stock.

This may be a dream.
Or perhaps not.
So I break the ox's glasses,
dig an ox-shaped hole in the garden
and later eat it medium rare
except for its tail
which I make into soup
and its head which I hide
in my neighbour's bed.

I take stock.

This may be a dream.
Or perhaps not.
So I wash my hands,
make a blessing
and stroll home;
en route I see a red heifer
clashing with a golden calf
on a yellow brick road.

I take stock.

This may be a dream.
Or perhaps not.
So I phone my rabbi
who invites me to discuss the matter
before a saged audience
of Talmudic statesmen
and the heads of ten
Ivy League
Yeshivot.

I take stock.

This may be a dream.
Or perhaps not.
So I gather my thoughts
and some socks
and fly to Minsk
where I'm to speak from the dock
once my rabbi's scrolled down
the biblical don'ts of bovine envy.
But I've forgotten
everything I knew.
So I just say moo
and escape
through scholarly confusion
to a cloakroom
with eighty long black coats
and one green anorak.

I take stock.

This may be a dream.
Or perhaps not.
So I go home to bed
but I can't sleep
as my neighbour's wailing
before a photo of his ox
taped to his wall.
I go to complain
but can't find my glasses
and fall down
a me-shaped hole
in my garden.

I take stock.

This may be a dream.
Or perhaps not.
So I call the rabbi
on my mobile
and say I'm in a hole
He says not you again,
it's three am.
I say rabbi just tell me –
is this is a dream?

My rabbi takes stock.

He says this may be a dream.
Or then again
perhaps not.

Conspiracy

Are you the man they call Grunfeld? I asked.
He said, some people call me Grunfeld.

Who calls you Grunfeld? I asked
He said, Katzenellenbogen calls me Grunfeld.

Are you in fact Grunfeld? I asked.
He said, I may be Grunfeld.

Why only may be? I asked.
He said, because I may not be Grunfeld.

Why not? I asked.
He said, because I may be Greenfield.

Are you Greenfield? I asked.
He said, I'm Greenfield if you're Appleyard.

And if I'm Apfelfeld? I asked.
He said, in that case I'm Grunfeld.

Meyer

A traditional
Jewish gangster,
he complained he was only
Public Enemy
Number Six.

He borrowed his craft
from the street of perpetual
shadow and rumble
and fire escapes, criss-crossing
like the stockings
in Rosie Herz's
kosher brothels.

A traditional
Jewish gangster,
he might have been a banker
but circumstances
didn't permit.

He spoke easy
but stayed sober
as he soared from the ghetto
on a champagne cork powered
by the Womens' Christian
Temperance Union.

A traditional
Jewish gangster,
his violin case
in fact contained
his violin.

Or so they thought.

He protected business,
lent to bakers,
advised tailors
and candlestick makers,
partnered butchers,
valued judges
but disdained garbage
and cement.

A traditional
Jewish gangster,
or the Mob's Financier
as the papers put it

but there was no flowercade
and no one came
except Harry and Max
from the old days
and Meyer Junior,
a banker, who inherited only
a Miami condo
and 17 hats.

A traditional
Jewish gangster,
he was a tough Jew
when there were few
but he never killed on Shabbos.
Unless he had to.

Protest

He arrived
at the embassy
with padlock, chain,
megaphone,
leaflets, placards,
fleece and hamper
but no umbrella.

So when it rained
in a change of plan
he chained a man
from Amnesty
to the railings
and went home.

V

With Respect

When they machine-gunned Sonny
on the causeway
it was done with respect.
Strictly business.
Nothing personal.

When they sent Luca Brasi
to sleep with the fishes
it was done with respect.
Strictly business.
Nothing personal.

When they chopped Lucchese
into lots of bits
it was done with respect.
Strictly business.
Nothing personal.

When they built an office block
above Little Vinnie
it was done with respect.
Strictly business.
Nothing personal.

When they shot the Don
at his favourite restaurant
but before he'd eaten,

that was personal.

Profiling a Killer

They profiled the killer
from a half eaten apple
found at the scene.

An eater of fruit
especially apples;
easily tempted,
easily bored.

The angle of his teeth
forensically spoke
of average height,
above average IQ.
His bite was forthright,
compensation they thought
for early abuse.

They traced the apple
to its original tree
and rebuilt it on screen
green and unbitten
and turned it around
three sixty degrees
and virtually sliced it.
Though not to the core.

Working from his saliva
they re-enacted his life,
those bingo nights,
those trips to the sea.
The budget was tight,
a low cost production
in black and white.
No lighting or sound.

After some years
they called in a mystic
who called in a psychic
who advised
this hadn't been murder

it was suicide.

The Cons and Pros of Death

No sandcastles
   No people stamping on sandcastles

No people
   No sewage

No bathing
   No bathtime

No time
   No timetables

No tables
   No wobbly tables

No jelly
   No jellyfish

No fish restaurants
   No fish eyes

No eyes
   No contact lenses

No contact
   No punches

No punch
   No hiccups

No cups of tea
   No milky tea

No milk floats
    No oil slicks

No waves
    No tidal waves

No sandcastles

His Black Line

It swirled around Kent,
his house, his wife
and often circled
the M25
to and from work.

It crossed the channel
to Calais for booze
that weekend in Boulogne
when the wipers broke
in a tropical storm.

It nipped up to Leeds
in the early years
to see her folks.
Twice they punctured
on the way home.

It slipped down to Bristol.
He couldn't bloody
remember why.
Perhaps it was football.
Perhaps that was a lie.

He watched the young chap
in the neighbouring bed
whose red life line
intricately twirled.
He reached across

and placed the chart
over his own.
Their lines ran out
on the black spot where
they'd crashed head-on.

Pandora's Box

I hear they found
Pandora's Box.

I hear this time
they took no chances.

I hear they summoned
an intelligent robot
to open the box
but he curled up
in a ball
behind a wall.

I hear they summoned
a less intelligent robot
who opened
Pandora's Box.

I hear they found
no anger or angst.
Just some bubble wrap.
But Pandora had burst
all the bubbles.

Hello?

In a sleeping office
a telephone rings
a modem crackles
a computer bleeps.

Hello? says the computer.
But there's no answer.
Hmm, thinks the computer
with a frown
and again it closes
its systems down.

All is quiet
but in fact
all is changed,
changed utterly.

Trojan B
has come to town.

Knightmare

Pinned down
on a black and white battleground
by a horse
and eight little men
with round heads
and no faces,
he screamed.

And in the depths of the castle
the queen said to her husband –
the bishop is having
his chess dream again

Einstein said: "When a man sits with a pretty girl for an hour, it seems like a minute. But let him sit on a hot stove for a minute and it's longer than any hour. That's relativity."

That's Relativity

A man sits with a pretty girl
- an hour seems like a minute
but to her, more like a week.
He scribbles her through his eureka brainclap,
    how he overpowered m and c.
She sends him out to make the tea.

A man sits on a hot stove
- a minute seems like an hour
but to her, more like a year.
He observes the kettle which never boils,
    displaced by his thermo-dynamic mass.
She sends him up to take a bath.

A man sits with a pretty girl
- an hour seems like a minute
but to her, more like eternity.
She says goodnight and disappears at e,
    where e equals twice the speed of light.
That's relativity.

Whatever

He said
    take your umbrella
    but never take umbrage
    or bear a grudge
    or bare your soul;
    never speak
    until spoken to;
    always take no
    for an answer;
    keep yourself
    to yourself;
    but don't be yourself,
    be someone else;
    don't do today
    what you could've done
    yesterday;
    never speculate
    other than
    to accumulate;
    and never ever
    say never say never.

She said
    whatever.

Once Seen

You
reading Angela's Ashes
last carriage
Camden Town
6pm Sunday.

Me
black T-Shirt
reading over your shoulder.

You
adjusting the angle
so I couldn't.

Me
saying hi.

You
pretending not to hear.

Me
nibbling your ear.

You
kicking me
and pushing me out.

Me
now living in
PO Box 643.

Can I come home now darling?

Where We are Now

The antechamber where the poet immersed in words and wine.		
The corridor where the poet approached on the appointed day.		
The start of the poem proper say some experts.	The start of the poem proper say other experts.	
A figment of a fragment from another poem of the same period.		
Closed for restoration and not reopening any time soon.	All that's left of this bit.	Added by a later and better poet all agree.
		A cell where the poet hid from the world and himself.
	The end until the poet changed his mind.	The end until the poet changed his mind again.
		The point where the poet opted for the mystique of an unfinished

Nothing

Nothing isn't
a black hole.

Nothing isn't
a reason for much ado.

Nothing isn't
a lack of things.

Nothing isn't
nothingness.

Nothing isn't
anything.

Nothing isn't
something.

Nothing isn't
what is
or isn't there
before or after
something.

Nothing isn't
is.

Nothing isn't
isn't.

Nothing.

Footnotes

Those actuarial ants,
they tug us down
to their mezzanine cellar,
back-stocked with labelled stacks
of noteworthy facts[1]

[1] and afterthoughts

Those crass masters
of terse
and merciless detail,
submerged like inelegant royals
such as Prince John[2]

[2] died of epilepsy 1919

Those nano–distractors,
in point of factors,
their inferior complex
deep-wracked with biblio
mania[3]

[3] see further below

Those avid dusters
and uncorkers
of learned sources,
the Aeneid and Euclid,
and Ovid[4]

[4] and Ibid

VI

Disclaimer

If you've been affected
by any issue
in this poem,
please send
a self addressed envelope
to yourself.

Consult a doctor
if you must
but don't call us;
we won't call you

because
having taken
legal advice
this poem
reserves its rights.

Any reference
to anything comprehensible
is entirely
unintentional

and all characters
are fictitious
including you
and us.